D0435528

A MATTER OF
CONSCIENCE
The Trial of Anne Hutchinson

A MATTER OF
CONSCIENCE
The Trial of Anne Hutchinson

by Joan Kane Nichols

Alex Haley, General Editor

Illustrations by Dan Krovatin

RSVP
**RAINTREE
STECK-VAUGHN**
P U B L I S H E R S
The Steck-Vaughn Company

Austin, Texas

Published by Steck-Vaughn Company.

Text, illustrations, and cover art copyright © 1993 by Dialogue Systems, Inc., 627 Broadway, New York, New York 10012. All rights reserved.

Cover art by Dan Krovatin

Printed in the United States of America
1 2 3 4 5 6 7 8 9 R 98 97 96 95 94 93 92

Library of Congress Cataloging-in-Publication Data

Nichols, Joan Kane.
    A matter of conscience: the trial of Anne Hutchinson/Joan Kane Nichols; illustrator, Dan Krovatin.
        p. cm—(Stories of America)
    Summary: Recounts Anne Hutchinson's struggle with the Puritan Church over its rigid theocratic control of the Massachuettes Bay Colony, her trial for heresy and sedition, and banishment from the colony.
    ISBN 0-8114-7233-7, — ISBN 0-8114-8073-9(softcover)
    1. Hutchinson, Anne Marbury, 1591–1643—Trials, litigation, etc.—Juvenile literature. 2. Trials(Heresy)—Massachusettes—Boston—Juvenile literature. 3. Trials (Sedition)—Massachusettes—Boston—Juvenile literature. 4. Puritans—Massachusettes—History—Juvenile literature. [1. Hutchinson, Anne Marbury, 1591–1643 2. Puritans. 3.Trials (Heresy) 4. Trials (Sedition) 5. Freedom of religion—History.] I. Krovatin, Dan, ill. II. Title. III. Series.
KF223.H86N53   1993
345.73'0288—dc20   92-18087
[347.305288]   CIP
                                                      AC

ISBN 0-8114-7233-7 (Hardcover)
ISBN 0-8114-8073-9 (Softcover)

Introduction
by Alex Haley, General Editor

This is not a story about religious freedom. It is, in fact, a story in which there is no religious freedom and very little religious tolerance. It is a story in which there is little tolerance of any kind. Why tell it then? Because sometimes bad examples can be as useful to us as good ones, sometimes even more useful.

The people in the story are all good people. They are filled with high ideals. And they are all very much alike, all English Puritans. Despite their common background and beliefs, their community becomes divided by conflict. They cannot allow what they need most—tolerance.

Today we are a nation of diversity. We are not all English Puritans. We are all colors, all religions, all backgrounds. If tolerance fails us, what will be the result? This story provides a clue.

*To Amy Lang, who introduced me to
Anne Hutchinson.*

Contents

1 Leaving Old England

John Cotton shivered inside the black cloak that covered his body and most of his face. Huddled in the shadows of the pier, he looked out to sea, straining his eyes to catch a glimpse of the *Griffin*. The thin red line of the sun rising on the eastern horizon slowly widened. Now he could make out the outline of the ship where it lay at anchor some way out in the harbor.

With one of his long, delicate hands John Cotton touched his wife's arm. Startled, Sarah gave a small cry, but he patted her arm reassuringly and pointed out to sea. She drew the hood of her cloak back a little from her face to gaze at the *Griffin*, with its white sails trembling in the breeze. Her husband smiled at her. If all went well, their child would be born on that ship.

If all went well. John Cotton cast a fearful look back over his shoulder. The stretch of English coastline behind him, shrouded in morning fog, was empty save for gulls that wheeled and screamed overhead. He listened intently for the sound of horses' hooves, and he peered through the fog for the sight of riders on lathered horses in hot pursuit. But he heard and saw nothing. So far, the plan had worked.

Ordinarily, passengers bound for the Massachusetts Bay Colony in New England boarded the *Griffin* at Wight, dozens of miles farther down the coast. But the Cottons had made arrangements with the captain of the *Griffin* to be picked up on this lonely coast instead, where the king's agents wouldn't expect them.

For twenty years, John Cotton had been the greatest Puritan minister in England. People everywhere had flocked to St. Botolph's in Boston to hear his brilliant sermons. Then, during the late 1620s, the agents of the new king, Charles I, began to silence and imprison Puritan ministers all over the country because Puritan beliefs did not conform to those of the established church.

At first, John Cotton had been pretty much left alone. Although he was questioned a few times about his religious beliefs, Cotton had a way of answering honestly but still sounding innocent. This talent, in times when plain speaking often landed one in prison or worse, served Cotton well. Nor was Cotton hurt by his great fame and many influential friends.

But even these protections failed when the persecutions increased. One day in October of 1632, he received an urgent message from a friend. The message said only, "Fly!"

Leaving his new wife behind, John Cotton fled. For nine months, disguised and using an assumed name, he ran like a fox fleeing the hounds. The king's agents stayed on his heels as he was chased from the home of one powerful friend after another. Eventually Sarah had joined him, and they had worked their way here to the southern coast of England and arranged secret passage on the *Griffin*. Now, if their plan worked, they would soon leave England behind and set off for the shelter of the American wilderness.

With the sun now well over the horizon, John and Sarah could begin to make out movement aboard the *Griffin*. As they watched, a small boat dropped over the ship's side and began cutting its way toward them. Once again John Cotton looked back over his shoulder. He saw no one. Their plan had worked.

Plowing steadily toward them, the boat reached the pier and nuzzled against it. Cotton handed their bundles and bags to the men in the boat, gently helped his wife to a seat, and slipped in beside her.

The strong arms of the rowers reversed the boat's direction, and it headed back toward the ship. John Cotton felt the tension leave his shoulders. He patted his wife's hand and smiled.

Leaving England and moving to a new country was sad and a bit frightening. But at least in America the agents of the king were few and far between. Puritans need not fear persecution there. The Massachusetts Bay Colony was, in fact, run by Puritans. Everyone shared the same beliefs and followed the same practices. There Cotton would be able to preach God's word openly and freely. In the new land across the ocean, a Puritan was free to speak the truth.

■ ■ ■

The person most responsible for the existence of the Massachusetts Bay Colony was John

Winthrop. Three years earlier, in 1630, Winthrop had sat proudly upon a platform with the other leaders of the expedition to America. They were waiting for the Reverend Cotton to deliver a farewell sermon to themselves and the rest of the colony's founders. Surveying the scene before him that cool, clear April day, John Winthrop had rubbed his hands with satisfaction. The great dream of his life was about to become a reality.

Outlined against the intense blue of the sky, he saw a fleet of full-masted sailing ships. The flagship, *Lady Arbella*, was in the lead, drawn up at anchor along the shore. A crisp breeze fluttered the ship's flags and brought to his nostrils the tangy smell of the sea.

Cluttering the shoreline were the last of the chests waiting to be loaded onto the ships. Each one carried a family's store of provisions for the months on board—meal, eggs in salt, peas, and other foods; pots and skillets for cooking; juice of scurvy grass and other medicines; a store of linen. The things they'd need once they reached America—horses and cows, farm tools and seed, a few necessary articles of furniture—were already safely stowed below decks.

All morning, Winthrop had overseen the preparations for departure. Hundreds of soon-to-be ships' passengers stood anxiously about. Among them, women in sober gowns of rich material, prosperous men in steeple hats and ruffs, craftspeople, soldiers, and servants. They had all scurried about taking care of last-minute details. Meanwhile their children, dressed like miniature versions of their parents, had jumped and played around the piles of goods. John Winthrop, almost bursting with happiness, had talked, consulted, answered questions, given directions, and generally shepherded everyone through the confusion.

But now the hubbub had quieted down. John Winthrop sat above the heads of the expectant crowd. In a few minutes John Cotton would deliver the farewell sermon. This was a moment for reflection, perhaps even a moment for doubt. Pulling thoughtfully on his narrow pointed beard, John Winthrop gazed down at the somber faces of the thousand people assembled below, the thousand people willing to sail with him across the ocean to a new home in the wilderness.

Like nearly everyone else in the country, Winthrop belonged to the kingdom's official church, the Church of England. Less than a hundred years before, during a time of great religious conflict in Europe, the Church of England had broken away from the Catholic Church.

Winthrop and his followers were among those who thought that the Church of England hadn't broken far enough away. They were called Puritans because they wanted to "purify" the Church of England. They wanted to simplify church ceremonies so they would be less like those of the Catholic Church. They also challenged the authority of church leaders. It was too much, they said, like the Catholic Church. Instead of the Pope,[1] the Church of England had the Archbishop of Canterbury and the king. Puritans believed that the Bible provided all the necessary guidance for governing church members. Ministers were important teachers, but final authority belonged to the Bible and to the conscience of the individual.

Because of these ideas, the Puritans often came into conflict with the leaders of the Church of England, particularly with the king himself. Just as the king had rejected the authority of the

---

[1] the head of the Catholic Church

Catholic Church a hundred years before, the Puritans seemed ready to reject the king's authority in religious matters.

Despite the conflicts, most Puritans still believed that reform would come to the Church of England in time. More than a few, however, felt that something more was needed. They wanted to make a fresh start in America, away from the problems and conflicts of England. In America, they would create a new community—one made up entirely of Puritans like themselves. It would serve as a model of reform for the Church of England.

Some might have considered migrating to America cowardly, an act of running away. Perhaps the brave thing, the right thing, was to stay and continue the struggle here at home. Some may have thought this, but not John Winthrop. Whatever his last-minute thoughts, Winthrop had solved that inner debate over a year ago. He had decided that he would serve God best by leading this purified model of the English church to America. There he would found a "New Jerusalem," a "City Upon a Hill," a model community to show the Puritans remaining in England what all of England could become.

Once more Winthrop fondly cast his eyes over the crowd of godly people below him. In such a society all would think and act as one. After all, were they not God's elect? Were they not God's chosen?

Gentle-faced John Cotton stood up to pray, and John Winthrop bowed his head. What greater honor could there be than to lead God's own people on such an errand into the wilderness? Winthrop could only pray that he would be worthy.

■ ■ ■

That April 8, 1630, when the Puritan fleet departed Southampton for New England, John Cotton had remained behind. He was one of those Puritans who had no intention of leaving England. Yet the dawn of this July day three years later found him and his wife being rowed across a lonely harbor to a ship that would take them to America.

The emigration of John Cotton, England's most popular minister, was a disappointment to many. To Anne Marbury Hutchinson of Lincolnshire, it was a disaster.

One day, soon after she heard the news, she sat inside the great hall of her manor house, pondering what she should do. Absent-mindedly, she

rocked the cradle by her side, hushing the infant within it. Her small children played quietly outside the door, but she hardly heard them. Her mind was intent on the well-worn Bible that lay upon her lap.

Anne Hutchinson was an independent thinker. Encouraged by her intelligence, her father had given her an education far superior to the one most girls received. Most of her thinking was about religion, and she'd become used to forming opinions and solving problems through her own reading and reflection. But she needed to know that at least some of the ministers of the church shared the same conclusions.

She recalled how she and William, her husband, had traveled about the countryside listening to different ministers preach. Most, she was convinced, taught falsehoods rather than truths. Then one day she'd heard John Cotton. From then on, as often as she could manage, she traveled the twenty-four miles—two days there and back on horseback—to listen to him preach.

Her brow furrowed. Now Cotton was gone. What should she do? Turning the pages of the Bible, she came upon this verse in Isaiah, "And though the Lord give you the bread of adversity,[2] and the water of affliction, yet shall not thy teachers be removed into any corner any more, but thine eyes shall see thy teachers."

The baby had fallen asleep. Anne Hutchinson stood up and placed the heavy Bible on a nearby table. She walked to the doorway and looked out at the hills dotted with grazing sheep. From the other side of the house came the laughter of her children playing at some game.

The scent of hawthorn blossoms filled the air. In the distance she could see the church tower that rose above the houses of the tiny village. She could feel the presence of the sea, not so many miles away.

Suddenly the answer to her question throbbed sharp and strong within her, as though God spoke directly to her heart. "The Lord is carrying Mr. Cotton to New England," she said, "I must go thither also."

---

[2] hardship

2 Arrival in Boston

It took Anne and William Hutchinson and their eleven children almost a year to get ready for their journey across the Atlantic Ocean. Edward, their eldest son, was sent on ahead to prepare for their arrival. By July of 1634, the Hutchinsons were on board the *Griffin*, the same ship that had carried John Cotton to America the year before.

After a few weeks of storms and seasickness, the weather turned calm and daily life settled into a routine. One day of cloudless blue sky followed another. The middle Hutchinson children—Samuel, Anne, Mary, and Katherine—joined the other children on board in running about the deck and playing games with the sailors. The older ones—Richard, Faith, Bridget, and Francis—helped their parents with the family's daily needs and took care of three-year-old William and baby Susanna. All listened to the sermons preached daily below decks.

Anne Hutchinson paid close attention to these sermons, but grew more and more distressed at what she heard, feeling that the sermons contained errors. One day, irritated beyond her endurance, she rose abruptly from her seat and, with a sleeping Susanna cradled over her shoulder, stormed up the brief flight of stairs to the upper deck. Faith and Bridget, little William in tow, trailed after her.

On deck Anne led her daughters to a sheltered spot near the fish tubs. A few barrels lay scattered about. Sitting down on one, Anne took several deep breaths, then shook her head in disbelief. She simply could not abide the distorted teaching of that Zachariah Symmes.

Above her the sun glinted through the masts and sails that towered overhead. A few stormy petrels flew by against a background of blue sky. Salt spray showered the air. Faith picked up William and positioned him so he could watch the fish swimming in the tubs.

From where Anne sat she could see Samuel, Anne, Mary, and Katherine swaying back and forth on the long rope that had been stretched from steerage to mainmast for the exercise and enjoyment of the children on board. Sailors were everywhere, busy with their work. A servant caught fighting yesterday stood in a corner, his hands bound to a bar. A basket of stones hung from his neck. Another sinner with tied hands was being forced to walk in circles around the deck.

These familiar sights of punishment for the wicked soothed Anne a little. They were a warning to those who would sin and a comfort to those who stayed faithful to God's laws. Encouraged by the presence of Puritan justice, Anne sent Bridget down to the cabins to fetch the family's torn linen and the sewing box. She might as well do something useful with her anger.

Why couldn't that Symmes have chosen another theme for his sermon? "The evidencing of a good estate" indeed! She looked at her oldest daughter and sighed. Faith patted her mother's hand in sympathy. It was, Anne knew, a subject on which so many ministers, even good ones, went astray.

"The evidencing of a good estate" meant finding in earthly proofs—such as church member-ship, business success, a reputation for good-ness—some sign of assurance that one would go to heaven. Puritans believed that God had chosen only a few people to be saved. All but these few were destined for eternal suffering in hell. Puritans, therefore, never tired of thinking, talk-ing, and praying about matters involving the assurance of salvation.

Anne, too, viewed it as an important topic. Didn't everyone want assurance of salvation? But you couldn't teach false doctrine simply to calm people's fears or ease their worries. It wasn't a topic for feeble minds. Reverend Cotton could address the subject clearly and precisely. Reverend Symmes could not.

Just then Bridget returned with the linen, interrupting Anne's thoughts. Then the three women were silent as they threaded their needles and set to work.

A few other women, curious about Anne's obvious dissatisfaction with the morning sermon, joined Anne and her daughters. The women had listened to Symmes's sermon to the end. Now, as they had before, they would listen to Anne Hutch-inson explain where Symmes had gone wrong.

One of the younger women was confused. She, too, wanted to be sure she was among the saved. She had already been admitted as a member of the church. Wasn't *that* a sign that she was saved? Anne shook her head. Church membership was only a partial sign, not a complete assurance.

The woman persisted. She obeyed the commandments, prayed every day, showed charity to others. Wasn't that enough?

Anne shook her head even harder. No. No. No. That was exactly the kind of external evidence that Symmes talked so much about—the evidence of works, of the good things you did with your life. But the real evidence was internal—an inward communion with Christ.

Anne smiled sweetly at the questioning woman. Had she experienced Christ dwelling within her?

Shyly, the woman nodded. Yes, she had.

Then that was all the evidence she needed. There was no better proof. Nothing else mattered.

The shadow of the Reverend Symmes loomed above them, his thin lips even thinner than usual, his grim expression revealing his thoughts. What was this woman preaching?

Anne looked up from her sewing. Symmes bowed his head stiffly in her direction. He had come to see if she was feeling well. She had rushed out so abruptly that he'd feared she had a touch of seasickness.

Crisply, she shook her head. She noted that only the women who stayed under hatches got sick. Like the men and the children, she preferred to stay in the wholesome air.

Anne turned back to her sewing, and the Reverend Symmes's brows drew together. Mistress Hutchinson had left before he finished his sermon. Didn't she find the word of God wholesome?

Anne's needle stilled, and she looked up quickly. Yes, the word of God was wholesome, but the words of the Reverend Symmes were troublesome. Anne's reply was tart. She and the other women had been discussing his sermon, she informed Symmes, and they had questions that needed answers.

Symmes grew stiff. Perhaps if Mistress Hutchinson had stayed to hear the end of his sermon her questions would be answered.

Mistress Hutchinson doubted it. Her needle

flashed again. She had noticed, for example, that Mr. Symmes seemed to dwell on external signs of salvation. But weren't those external signs—those good works—unreliable? Anyone could behave well. What did that prove? Didn't the Bible say as much in many, many places?

Symmes colored. Only ministers could interpret scripture correctly, not a layman. Certainly not a *laywoman*.

Anne Hutchinson again looked up from her sewing. Did he not know John Cotton, he who had been the finest minister in England? Hadn't Cotton himself said he wouldn't want Christians to find assurance from good works, but only "such as floweth from faith in Christ Jesus"?

Symmes sputtered, unable to answer. He didn't wish to argue if or how his own beliefs differed from John Cotton's. Especially not in front of a women's sewing circle.

Baby Susanna stirred and began to whimper. Handing her mended linen to Bridget, Anne Hutchinson stood up. She must go down to the cabins now and feed her child. Gazing into Symmes's eyes, she said, "When we come to Boston, you'll see that there is something beyond the things you preach." As a parting shot, she added, quoting some words of Christ, "I have yet many things to say unto you, but ye cannot bear them now."

At that piece of presumption, Zachariah Symmes stalked off, red-faced and fuming. Faith gazed after his retreating back.

Three weeks later, on another bright sunny day, the lookout sighted land. The weary passengers aboard the *Griffin* stumbled to their feet and hurried above decks. They were eager to catch their first glimpse of their new home as their ship streamed into Boston harbor.

After two months of danger, sickness, boredom, and the stench of cattle in the hold—mixed with that of their own unwashed bodies—the voyage was at last over. Everyone was overjoyed to see solid earth at last. And after months of miserable food—ship biscuit, dried peas, salt meat, stale water, and sour beer—they could hardly wait for their first fresh food and drink in months.

Along with the rest of the pushing, shoving passengers, the Hutchinsons made their way to the side of the ship. They pressed themselves against the bulwarks. Wind beat against their faces, choking the breath in their mouths and stinging their eyes with tears. Huddling together, they pointed and shouted as the Boston peninsula loomed larger and larger before them.

They passed islands dotting the harbor. Deep coves along the shoreline grew deeper as they approached. Hills rose higher and higher. Now they could make out the flat wet sands of the beach, the bleak marshes choked thick with grass, the flat pastures, the straggling line of drab gray houses.

They saw few trees, though across the back bay separating Boston from the rest of the colony there were trees enough. Forests teeming with savage beasts surrounded each tiny Puritan village in the colony.

The children crowded around their parents as the ship dropped anchor. Samuel, Anne, Mary, and Katherine were all in danger of falling overboard from sheer excitement. Even little William struggled in his father's arms. Only baby Susanna slept quietly in her mother's embrace as Anne scanned the faces of the people lining the shore. Suddenly she spotted her son Edward and waved frantically.

Docking was all confusion. The sailors up in the rigging shouted out instructions. Huge wooden cranes deposited casks, chests, crates, and barrels on the shore. The Hutchinsons and other passengers stumbled over ropes and sacks of grain as they gathered possessions and rounded up children.

Anne Hutchinson ushered her family ashore. The routine horrors of the journey were behind her. She had only good things to look forward to now. She would be reunited with her oldest son. She would have a secure home in the new community that its founder, John Winthrop, was calling a "City Upon a Hill," and a "New Jerusalem." Best of all, she would soon be seeing and hearing the brilliant John Cotton again.

But among the passengers going ashore that day, there was one who could and would cause trouble for Anne Hutchinson. The Reverend Zachariah Symmes was still angry with Anne Hutchinson for arguing with him over the meaning of his shipboard sermons. With no proper womanly modesty at all, this *woman* had dared to dispute his sermons. In front of everyone she had lectured him on his sermons!

He was determined to speak to the authorities about her. A woman like Anne Hutchinson could cause real trouble in the colony. Without a backward glance, he was off the boat and asking the way to the governor's house.

3 One of the Elect

A few days later, in the peace of the Sabbath morning, the Hutchinsons, scrubbed clean of two months' worth of grime, set out down the dusty paths of Boston. William, freshly shaved, walked beside Anne. Both clasped psalm books in their hands.

The Hutchinson children followed behind in orderly rows. Faith and Bridget took turns carrying baby Susanna. Even little William, minding his manners, walked quietly along as the family wended its way through Boston. Ahead of them stood the square one-story cabin, thatched with marsh grass and sealed with mud, that was the church meetinghouse.

It was a crisp, clear autumn day, more beautiful than any autumn day that Anne had ever seen before. Beyond the edge of town, the forest trees glowed red and burnished gold. Other family groups clustered in front of the meetinghouse. Anne and William nodded to their new neighbors. Most were strangers, but meeting and talking here every First-day,[3] they would become friends.

The Hutchinsons entered the meetinghouse. They walked up the aisle past the indentured servants and American Indians and African slaves who sat in the back rows, past the ordinary people who sat in the middle rows, and up to the front. William Hutchinson was a successful merchant. His family would sit in the front where, as prosperous, well-to-do members of the community, they belonged. Facing them were the church elders, the deacons, and the magistrates,[4] who sat on either side of the pulpit.

William and the older boys sat on one side of the aisle. Anne, the girls, and the younger boys sat on the other. All sat on the same kind of backless wooden benches.

---

[3] Sunday
[4] local government officials

Anne Hutchinson settled into her seat with satisfaction. This was what she had dared the terrors of the wilderness for. Here there would be no fear of the king's agents forcing the ministers of truth into hiding. Here they could freely preach as they saw fit. Here at last she could listen to the golden voice of Mr. Cotton, a voice she had not heard for over two years.

But before she could hear John Cotton, Anne had to sit through three turns of the hourglass as dry-faced, dry-mouthed, dry-spoken John Wilson, the other minister of the Boston church, droned his way through the morning sermon. After a break for a cold dinner, afternoon services began. Only then did Anne again feel that old stirring of her heart and mind as she listened to John Cotton preach the familiar doctrine she had waited so long to hear.

Many people seemed to find his words difficult to understand. But they were clear to her. John Cotton taught that salvation didn't come from anything you could do yourself. Salvation couldn't be gained by going to church, or by saying prayers, or even by being honest, upright, hard-working, or kind to one's neighbors. All these things were admirable, of course. And while

the saved did have all of these characteristics, so did many who weren't saved.

Good behavior neither earned you salvation nor was proof that you were chosen by God. To rely on good works for proof of salvation was to be under a Covenant of Works. This was the Catholic idea that through good works alone one could earn one's way to heaven.

John Cotton preached that salvation came only as a free gift from God. God chose whom he would save and whom he would damn, and there was nothing anyone could do about it. God bestowed grace on only a few.

This doctrine was called the Covenant of Grace, and supposedly all Puritans believed in it. Yet some ministers that Anne had heard—like Zachariah Symmes, who had preached on board ship—seemed to lean dangerously close to preaching the Covenant of Works. But not John Cotton.

When services were over for the day, people slowly got up, stretched and blinked, and turned to leave. Although everyone in the colony was required to attend services, most of the people filing through the meetinghouse door weren't members of the church. Some had never applied for membership. Others had applied before and been turned down.

For Anne Hutchinson there was no question about whether to apply. The church was made up of the saved. And Anne knew that she was one of the elect.

William and Anne Hutchinson applied for church membership at once. Within a few weeks, first William and then Anne were examined by the church elders to make sure that each was fit for admission. Had she received the call from God, Anne was asked, that indicated she was one of his chosen few? Did she know and accept the beliefs of the Puritan faith? Was she willing to obey the rules of the church and be guided by its leaders?

On October 26, 1634, William was informed that he'd been admitted to the Boston church. For Anne there was no such message. This was strange. Married couples were usually admitted into membership together. What could be wrong?

The week dragged on. Still no word. One by one other newly arrived couples were received into the bosom of the church. Of the applicants, only Anne remained outside. A small spark of fear burned inside her. Suppose, after all, they simply refused to let her join?

Not to join the church! The thought clutched at her heart. The church was more than a place to practice religion, more than a body of believers united in one faith. Joining the church was like becoming part of a large family. Why else had she given up her home and traveled to this strange wild land? Why this delay?

The waiting was unbearable.

At the end of the week, a message arrived for Mistress Hutchinson. She was summoned to a special meeting at the governor's house for questioning. What could this mean? Anne knew she'd already answered all the appropriate questions. What more could they ask? Controlling her anxiety as best she could, Anne walked down the high road to the house of Thomas Dudley, governor of the colony this year.

Governor Dudley welcomed Anne to his house. Then he directed her to a small study off to the side. The ministers would be questioning her, he said. Clad in her best gray gown, she strode into the room, back straight, head erect. Facing her were Pastor John Wilson, looking somber and severe, her own saintly John Cotton—and the Reverend Zachariah Symmes.

With level eyes, Anne Hutchinson looked into

Mr. Symmes's face. Now she was beginning to understand the reason for the delay. Why hadn't she thought of him before? She took a deep breath. Let him say what he would. She wasn't afraid. She had said and done nothing wrong.

Mr. Symmes had much to say. To start, he accused Anne of making prophecies.

Prophecies? Anne was taken aback. This was nearly the same as accusing her of being a witch! She sat up straight and glared at Symmes. What prophecies?

Symmes pointed an accusing finger. Did she remember that time during their journey when everyone had grown heartily sick of life at sea? Hadn't she said to a weary passenger, "What would you say if we should be at New England within these three weeks?"

What a fool this man was! Did he think she was a witch because of *that*? Yes, she admitted, she had made that comment, but. . . .

And she'd been right, too, Symmes interrupted, as though being right made everything worse.

But most offensive of all, he went on, she'd questioned his teaching. His sermons on the "evidencing of a good estate," for example. If God chose you, he'd explained to the passengers on the

Griffin, you would of course become a better person. Your behavior would improve. This improved behavior would be a sign that you were saved.

Mistress Hutchinson had argued with him about that. Anyone could behave well, she'd said. Even pagans and Catholics. What did that prove? According to Mistress Hutchinson the only way to be sure of salvation was in the way her teacher John Cotton taught—by internal evidence. Did you experience Christ dwelling within you? Then you were saved.

Finally, Symmes continued, Mistress Hutchinson hadn't even bothered to listen to his answers. Wait till he heard what John Cotton had to say. "When we come to Boston," Symmes reported her saying, anger returning as he spoke, "you'll see that there is something beyond the things you preach."

And if that wasn't enough, Symmes concluded, she'd actually said to him, "I have yet many things to say to you, but ye cannot bear them now." Rebuking him, a minister of the Lord, with Christ's own words! The effrontery!

As he finished speaking, Symmes recovered himself and smiled smugly, daring Mistress Hutchinson to contradict his words.

But she didn't deny anything. Instead, secure in her teacher's support, she appealed to Reverend Cotton. Wasn't it true, she asked him, that what she'd said to Mr. Symmes was only what Cotton himself had said many times before?

Gravely, Cotton nodded. Yes, he said, that was true. Turning to the others he explained his position on the "evidencing of a good estate." Mistress Hutchinson had only interpreted what he had often preached.

Anne Hutchinson allowed herself a brief triumphant smile. John Cotton had stood by her, as she'd known he would. Perhaps the colony wasn't perfect as she had at first hoped. But she needn't fear the spite of small minds. With Cotton here to back her up, she need never fear to speak the truth as she saw it.

For the moment, Anne had won. John Cotton was the leading minister in the colony. No one cared to dispute his words. Even Symmes, spite still glinting in his eyes, clamped his mouth shut. On November 2, Anne Hutchinson was admitted to membership in the Boston church.

4 Settling In

At the beginning of 1635 Pastor Wilson set sail for a year's visit to England. Now John Cotton was the only minister of the Boston church. Just as he had in old Boston, he drew large crowds of people to hear him preach. His Sunday services were jammed.

Soon he began delivering long public lectures on Thursday market days as well. Not only in Boston but in many of the surrounding towns and villages of the Bay colony—Newtown, Salem, Roxbury, Dorchester—people dropped their work and crowded to his lectures. In fact, so many days of work were lost, the magistrates had to pass a

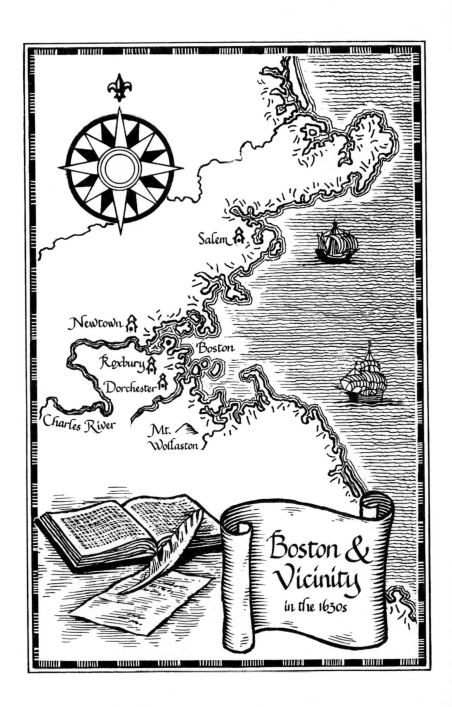

Salem

Newtown

Roxbury
Dorchester

Boston

Charles River

Mt.
Wollaston

Boston &
Vicinity
in the 1630s

law stating that no lectures could begin before one o'clock in the afternoon.

People enjoyed Cotton's preaching but didn't always understand it. They needed someone to make his meaning clear to them. They found that person in Anne Marbury Hutchinson.

The Hutchinsons had settled quickly into their place among the leading citizens of the Massachusetts Bay Colony. They built a large, two-story wooden house in the center of Boston, a few steps from the town spring, the meeting-house, and the market place.

Directly across the street was the house of John Winthrop and his wife Margaret. Even though he was not governor this year, Winthrop was still the leader of the Puritan community and would do anything to help it succeed. From her window Anne sometimes saw him, dressed in the plain clothes of an ordinary working man, work-ing at the same chores as his servants.

Not far away from the Hutchinson and Winthrop houses were the homes of John and Sarah Cotton and other well-to-do gentlemen and ladies, wealthy merchant families, and communi-ty leaders.

William Hutchinson was elected deputy to the General Court. Anne went from house to house using her nursing and midwife skills to help women who were ill or in childbirth. Soon she felt as well-loved in the new England as she had been in the old.

But not everyone was as fond of Anne Hutchinson as she thought. One day, as she waited at the bedside of a woman in labor, she sensed that the other women who had come to help were avoiding her eyes. When she went into the main room to get warm water from the pot that hung over the fireplace, she heard murmurings and mutterings follow her as she passed by.

Anne retreated to the bedchamber and laid down the pan of water on a table near the laboring woman's bed. Sitting down beside her, she dipped a cloth in the water, wrung it out, and wiped the woman's forehead. The woman smiled briefly in gratitude, then nodded off into a half sleep.

Anne looked across the bed at Mary Dyer sitting opposite and nodded in the direction of the dozing woman. It would be a while yet before she gave birth. Both women rose from the bedside and moved to chairs placed near the window.

Anne wanted to talk. She spread her strong, capable hands across her lap and leaned forward.

Her troubled glance searched her friend's grave, intelligent face. Why did the other women in the house resent her?

Mary Dyer hesitated a moment before answering. During the past few months, she and Anne Hutchinson had performed nursing duties at many a household together and had become close friends. The two women had much in common. Both cared deeply about religious matters and shared a similar belief in the indwelling spirit of God. Mary felt she owed it to her friend to speak frankly.

"Some women say you're too proud."

Anne was taken aback. Too proud? How was she proud? she wanted to know.

"It's about the women's meetings," Mary said. "They think you're too proud to attend the weekly meetings with the other women."

Anne sat back in her chair. Now she understood. Both men and women, she knew, often gathered in someone's house to discuss the week's sermons. But from what she'd heard, the women's meetings were often little more than gossip sessions. She had no desire to attend them. Yet she didn't want the women of Boston to resent her or to think she was too proud.

Anne thought for a moment. She wouldn't go to these meetings, she decided. She had a better idea. She would hold meetings in her own house instead. It would be a chance to review John Cotton's sermons and hold real discussions about the spiritual truths which burned inside her soul and mind.

And so one night a week later, a small group of lanterns bobbed in the darkness outside the Hutchinsons's thatch-roofed house. The door opened and Anne Hutchinson ushered her guests inside. Faith and Bridget helped the women off with their cloaks and invited them to sit on the benches and stools clustered in the center of the large room.

Anne seated herself in the room's only chair, facing her guests. Her back was to the hearth. She began speaking, repeating in her own words the sermon John Cotton had preached the Sabbath before. As she spoke, the light from the fireplace cast her shadow upward on the whitewashed wall.

After she stopped speaking, she answered questions and explained difficult passages. Many of the women, like her friend Mary Dyer and her neighbors—Mary Coggeshall, Elizabeth

Aspinwall, and Anne Leverett—were eager to learn. They grasped her points quickly.

A few, like the midwife Jane Hawkins, were there mainly for the warmth and sociability. But Anne was gracious to everyone. "Is that quite clear to you?" she asked, after explaining a particularly difficult point.

Goody Hawkins nodded her head. "Oh, yes, quite clear," she said.

Anne Hutchinson sometimes added her own emphasis to what Cotton had preached. For example, Cotton taught that good works weren't sufficient proof of salvation. Anne went a little further. She said they were useless. She taught that only one's inner certainty of a union with the Holy Spirit could give true assurance.

Also, although she didn't say so outright, Anne Hutchinson let it be known that she thought most of the other ministers leaned too far toward a belief in the Covenant of Works. Only John Cotton, she implied, truly preached the Covenant of Grace.

Because she spoke so well and explained things so clearly, her meetings quickly grew in size. Soon as many as sixty women were attending every week. Then men heard about the meetings. They wanted to come too, although for a woman to teach men was highly unusual, if not, according to Puritan customs, downright wrong. However, in no time, she was holding two meetings a week, one for women, the other for women and men together.

Anne drew people to her by the force of her personality and strong convictions. But not everyone saw the same truths Anne Hutchinson did. And a few, like John Winthrop, had no desire to attend her meetings. From his study window, Winthrop could look across the street and watch the twice-weekly comings and goings of Boston's Puritans. Each time he watched, he saw their numbers increase. And each time he watched, he became more and more uneasy.

As Winthrop walked through the Boston streets, he heard Anne Hutchinson's name on everyone's lips, including the barber-surgeon's. Whenever he sat down in William Dinely's chair for a haircut, Winthrop was treated to a discussion about Mistress Hutchinson's latest talk.

He heard about the man who brought new recruits to Anne Hutchinson's meetings. "Come along with me," this admirer would say, grabbing a passerby by the arm. Then, showing a fine disrespect for the colony's well-educated minis- ters, he would add, "I'll bring you to a woman that preaches better gospel than any of your blackcoats that have been at the ninneversity."

The more John Winthrop heard these things, the worse his uneasiness became. As far as he knew, Anne Hutchinson taught nothing wrong. His own wife Margaret attended some of the meetings and reported that Anne simply explained Cotton's sermons, though she did emphasize the doctrine of the inner voice of God speaking to each person in the privacy of his or her own soul.

Winthrop accepted this doctrine, too; he just didn't trust its emphasis. How could one be sure that the inner voice was really the voice of God? How could one be sure that it would say the same thing to each person to whom it spoke?

Emphasizing such a doctrine, he thought, endangered the community. How could everyone be kept on the same path if each person were to act on the prompting of an inner voice? If all authority came from within, what order would there be without? Sin would be everywhere. Disorder and lawlessness would rule.

If Anne Hutchinson knew of Winthrop's dismay, it left her unconcerned.

However, when John Wilson returned from England, he was very much concerned. Reverend Wilson discovered that just about his entire congregation—all but six or seven members of the Boston church—was devoted to John Cotton and Anne Hutchinson. Even Henry Vane, the new governor of the colony, had joined the circle of Anne Hutchinson's followers.

Wilson conferred with Winthrop. They were worried, and they weren't alone. The ministers of the churches of Dorchester, Roxbury, Salem, and other surrounding towns shared the alarm felt by Wilson and Winthrop. The ideal community of saints was falling apart. Anne Hutchinson and her followers were undermining the leadership of the colony and the Puritan church.

Something had to be done. John Winthrop watched and waited for a chance to bring Anne Hutchinson and her followers into line before things grew completely out of hand.

5 Between Truth and Error

By the fall of 1636, even Anne had to recognize that a serious controversy had erupted over her meetings. The sides were clearly drawn among the inhabitants of Massachusetts Bay Colony. On one side was Anne Hutchinson and the Boston congregation. On the other were John Winthrop, most members of the General Court, Pastor John Wilson, and the ministers and congregations of most of the surrounding towns. Only John Cotton refused to take sides.

Winthrop's first chance to take action came several months after John Wheelwright, Anne's brother-in-law, arrived from England. The members of the Boston church welcomed Wheelwright wholeheartedly. Here was another minister who preached the doctrines they believed in.

The Hutchinsonians wanted Wheelwright to be Cotton's fellow minister instead of John Wilson. Their attempt to install him in the church gave Winthrop the chance he'd been waiting for. All important church decisions had to be unanimous. Only one vote was needed to block Wheelwright's installation. Winthrop voted no.

Wheelwright was appointed to a smaller church at nearby Mount Wollaston. But the Hutchinsonians were still furious. Now it was their turn to feel that something must be done. They had no interest in listening to Wilson, or ministers like him, preach the false doctrines that smelled so much of the Covenant of Works. But church attendance was compulsory. They were forced to sit through the long sermons they found so hateful to their ears.

Then Anne Hutchinson and the other women came up with a plan. The next Sabbath day, when Wilson got up to preach, Anne got up too. She walked to the back of the church. A church official known as the tithing man was posted there to keep people from leaving. Anne murmured something about not feeling all that well, and left. How could the tithing man stop her? If she was sick, he had to let her leave.

Other women began doing the same. Some, with children in their arms, said their babies were cranky or needed feeding. Others claimed illness or other emergencies. The tithing man had to let them all out.

Sometimes, instead of leaving, Anne and her followers, both men and women, waited until Wilson finished his sermon. Then they stood up and questioned him. They demanded that he explain certain points he had made. Questioning the minister was allowed. But before it had always taken the form of praising the minister's sermon. The Hutchinsonians were attacking it.

Anne Hutchinson's ideas were popular in Boston. In the churches outside of Boston, the ideas of ministers like Wilson and Symmes held sway. A group of Hutchinsonians took turns attending services at neighboring churches. After each sermon, they rose and challenged the minister's sermon.

The split between the two groups worsened daily. Several ministers whose churches had been visited by Hutchinsonians called a meeting at John Cotton's house. They'd had enough. To this meeting they summoned Mistress Hutchinson.

Anne entered the house warily. Cotton was the only one present that she fully trusted. John Wilson presided. He and the other ministers acted very friendly. They assured her they only wanted to ask some questions privately, just for their own information. She should feel free, they insisted, to speak openly. They wanted to hear her opinions. For example, she'd said there was a difference between what John Cotton preached and what the other ministers preached. What did she mean by that?

Anne hesitated before answering. She knew she was in a dangerous spot. Seeing her hesitation, the Reverend Hugh Peter, a squarely built, outspoken man, said, "I pray answer the question directly, as fully and as plainly as you desire we should tell you our minds. Mrs. Hutchinson, we come for plain dealing and telling you our hearts."

Anne wasn't fooled by his words, though they sounded sincere. She was frightened. But then, half to herself, she said, "The fear of man is a snare. Why should I be afraid?" She looked into their faces. "It is true," she said. "There is a wide difference between you and Mr. Cotton."

John Cotton rubbed his hand across his chin. He wasn't sure he liked this. He felt himself to be in a delicate position. Only recently he too had been questioned by his fellow ministers about his beliefs. Happily he'd been able to convince them that his beliefs were substantially the same as theirs.

John Cotton liked being the leading minister in the colony, the one that Winthrop and the other officials relied on. He had no desire to risk his position. "I could have wished," he said to Anne, "that you had not put that in."

One of the other ministers asked her what she thought this difference was. Anne answered frankly. They preached that good works were a sign of salvation. Cotton preached that God's grace, freely given, was the only *certain* sign.

John Cotton was getting more and more uncomfortable. "I am very sorry," he said, "that you put comparisons between my ministry and theirs. You have said more than I could myself."

"I find the difference," she replied.

As one of them, Thomas Welde, took notes, the ministers continued their questioning. How was their teaching different from Cotton's? they wanted to know. She told them. One at a time they asked her, "And what about me, Mistress Hutchinson? How do I preach?"

She answered each one.

But try as they might they couldn't trap her into saying anything for which she could be punished. She stopped short of saying any of them preached a Covenant of Works. All she would admit to was believing they didn't preach the Covenant of Grace as clearly as Cotton or Wheelwright did.

A day of fasting and prayer was declared for January 20, 1637. Perhaps this would begin to heal the wounds within the colony. In Boston, Reverend Wilson delivered the morning sermon as usual. But in the afternoon someone asked young John Wheelwright to speak "as a private brother."

Wheelwright, a brisk, determined, forthright man, strode to the pulpit. He would speak his mind, never mind the consequences. The sermon he delivered was not a healing one. He refused to whitewash the differences between the two sides. Instead he sought to rally the Hutchinsonians and rebuke their rivals.

In strong and fiery language, he defended their beliefs and warned them of the danger they were facing if they shrunk from the truth. "When enemies to the way of truth oppose the way of God, we must lay hold upon them, we must kill them with the word of the Lord."

No, not a healing word or thought from this quarter, but what of it! Even if this was, in Wheelwright's uncompromising words, to "cause a combustion[5] in church and commonwealth," then so it must, for "did not Christ come to send fire upon the earth?"

"We must all of us prepare for battle," he shouted, "and come out against the enemies of the Lord; and if we do not strive, those under a Covenant of Works will prevail."

John Winthrop could hardly be pleased at the way things were going. Things were getting worse, not better. Wheelwright's sermon had done nothing to calm the troubled waters. In fact, he had done what Anne Hutchinson had refused to do before the ministers. He had accused them of teaching heresy,[6] of teaching the Covenant of Works. They, in turn, would accuse him of sedition.[7]

---

[5] explosion
[6] false or misleading religious instruction
[7] calling for rebellion against legal authority

When the General Court met on March 9, 1637, it found Wheelwright guilty of sedition and contempt for reviling the colony's ministers. A petition of protest was raised by 75 Hutchinsonians, most of them from Boston. The Court rejected the petition and announced it would pass sentence on Wheelwright later.

In May of that year, Winthrop succeeded in regaining the governor's seat from Henry Vane. Next he wanted to take back control of the Boston church from the Hutchinsonians. For this he would need help.

On the 30th of August, a gathering of 25 ministers, elders, and lay members of all the churches in the colony met to review Puritan teachings. Their purpose was to make up a list of the erroneous opinions that were floating around the colony and denounce them.

They identified 82. No one at this first New England synod[8] *said* that these were errors that Anne Hutchinson taught. But everyone *knew* that that was what they meant.

The line between truth and error was a fine one, as John Cotton had continuously demon-

---

[8] assembly of church leaders to discuss matters of faith

strated. Too fine for some. If there was one point that opponents like Symmes and Wheelwright might agree on, it was this. The time had come to choose between truth and error.

Winthrop had chosen. What Anne Hutchinson believed and John Wheelwright preached, in Winthrop's mind, was heresy. The synod's list would force people to choose. Even reluctant John Cotton had chosen finally, agreeing to condemn the teachings and practices identified on the list of errors.

Cotton's endorsement would bring many members of the Boston church to heel. In November, the General Court took care of Reverend Wheelwright, banishing him from the colony. They also punished anyone who had signed the petition of protest on Wheelwright's behalf. Among these was Edward Hutchinson, Anne's brother-in-law.

A hard and bitter peace was being enforced on the colony.

Anne Hutchinson remained to be dealt with. The synod had condemned both the practice of challenging ministers in church and meetings led by women that discussed "questions of doctrine." Such meetings, the synod concluded, were "disorderly and without rule." Both findings were directed at Anne.

But the synod's findings on these matters were more along the lines of recommendations than rules. Church members need only take them under advisement, not obey them. Anne and her followers ignored them. They continued to challenge ministers' sermons, and she continued to hold her weekly meetings.

Something more was needed. Evidence of heresy or sedition would bring Anne Hutchinson down, as it had Wheelwright. Everyone knew what Anne Hutchinson believed, but she couldn't be punished for her beliefs, only for her words or actions. John Winthrop summoned her before the Court. He would find her guilt, if it could be found.

6 The Trial Begins

On the day in November appointed for her trial, Anne Hutchinson woke up early to dark skies and a biting cold. After a quick breakfast, she wrapped a shawl over her cloak, and with her husband by her side, she stumbled through the icy Boston streets. A boat waited at the river to take them across to Newtown. Chunks of ice clogged the river's gray waters. Anne sat huddled in her seat. Her bones grew numb with cold, as much from dread as from the weather.

Thin ice covered the rungs of the ladder on the Newtown side. Climbing would be treacherous. Anne went up first. William followed closely

behind her. She slipped once, then steadied herself, pulling herself up rung by icy rung.

Drifts of hard-packed snow lay along the forest path leading to Newtown village. Despite the weakness she felt, Anne stepped along bravely. She would need all her wit and courage today. Steeling herself for the ordeal to come, she felt her mind and heart sharpen and grow strong.

Inside the tiny meetinghouse, a watery wash of dim winter light filtered through the small leaded windows. Crowds of people jammed the hard benches. Puffs of icy breath rose above their heads. The smell of damp wool filled the cold air. Even though the trial was in Newtown, Mary Dyer and a number of Anne's supporters from Boston managed to attend.

A long table stretched across the front of the room. Magistrates sat along one end, ministers along the other. In the center sat Governor Winthrop, fixing Anne Hutchinson with an icy stare as she walked up the aisle to face the Court.

John Cotton sat quietly to one side, his hands folded in front of him, looking as though he wished he were anywhere but here.

Anne gazed at each man at the front table in turn. On one side of Winthrop sat wild-eyed John Endicott of Salem. On the other side was Deputy-

Governor Thomas Dudley, a man whose view of Anne Hutchinson was extreme. Dudley believed she was deluded by the devil. Next to Endicott were gruff, energetic Hugh Peter, grim-faced John Wilson, and nervous little Thomas Welde. Anne also spied her old enemy Zachariah Symmes, who seemed to be gloating at her.

Facing Anne Hutchinson at the long table were the men who would be her prosecutors, judges, and jury all in one. Of the ministers, she knew that only John Cotton was on her side. Among the magistrates who sat with Dudley and Winthrop, only William Coddington and William Colburn were sympathetic. She had no lawyer but herself.

"Mistress Hutchinson," Governor Winthrop began, as the buzz of conversation quieted down, "you are called here as one of those that have troubled the peace of the commonwealth and the churches here. You are known to be a woman that hath had a great share in the promoting and divulging of those opinions that are causes of this trouble."

In the stern voice of authority, he went on to accuse her of having friends and relatives among the guilty, of insulting the churches and their ministers, of continuing to hold public meetings even after the synod had declared against them.

He paused and narrowed his eyes. Then he set the terms clearly before her. Either she submitted to the authority and judgment of the Court or she'd be thrown out of the colony. How did she answer to the charges? he asked.

In a strong, clear voice she replied, "I am called here to answer before you, but I hear no things laid to my charge."

"I have told you some already and more I can tell you," Winthrop snapped back.

"Name one, Sir."

"Have I not named some already?"

She requested he be specific. "What have I said or done?"

She'd been friendly to Wheelwright and those who supported him, Winthrop argued.

Her voice rang out. "That's a matter of conscience, Sir." A few muffled cheers broke out behind her. Even in Puritan Boston, people had the right to their opinions, as long as they weren't expressed.

"Your conscience you may keep to yourself," Winthrop replied. But, he continued, if her conscience had led her to approve of those who broke the law, that was an action for which she could be punished.

She wanted to know what law her friends had broken. "The law of God?" she asked.

"Yes, the Fifth Commandment, which commands us to honor father and mother, and this includes the fathers of the commonwealth."

But suppose the children were wiser than the fathers, she countered. Suppose they honored the Lord better than their fathers did? Would it be wrong for her to approve of the children because the fathers of the commonwealth forbid it? Anne saw her friend William Coddington nod his head. She'd made a good point.

"That's nothing to the purpose," Winthrop thundered. This woman was getting the better of him, and he liked it no more than Reverend Symmes had liked it. "We do not mean to discourse with those of your sex," he said sharply.

He repeated the charge. Because she was friendly with Wheelwright and the others, she had dishonored the fathers of the community.

But Anne Hutchinson would not accept that. "I do acknowledge no such thing. Neither do I think that I ever put any dishonor upon you."

Realizing that he was getting nowhere, Winthrop shifted to another charge. "What say you to your weekly public meetings?"

"There were such meetings in use before I came," Anne answered. "We began it with but five or six, and though it grew to more in future time, yet being tolerated at the first, I knew not why it might not continue."

"There were private meetings indeed," Winthrop agreed. "And are still in many places, of some neighbors, but not so public and frequent as yours. Yours are of another nature. But answer by what authority, or rule, you uphold them."

Winthrop was asking her to show a Biblical example that would give a woman the right to hold public meetings. Unfortunately, the Bible offered few examples, if any, that would satisfy Winthrop's notion of proof.

But she did her best. "By Titus 2, where the elder women are to teach the younger," she said, referring to a book in the Bible.

Winthrop pounced. "So we allow you to do. As the apostle there names—privately." Besides, he went on, she didn't teach women what Titus says she should teach them—to stay at home.

She asked whether any part of the Bible actually forbade what she did. "Will you please to give me a rule against it, and I will yield," she said.

But no, the game didn't work that way. "You must have a rule *for* it," Winthrop insisted, "or else you cannot do it."

Then he thought of something. "Yet you have a plain rule against it." He recited the Biblical sentence he'd just remembered. "I permit not a woman to teach."

His smugness angered Anne. "Do you think it not lawful for me to teach women?" she shot back. "And why do you call me to teach the Court?"

Frustration brought tears to her eyes. The unfairness of the proceedings suddenly seemed like a burden too heavy to bear. Wearily, she slumped against the table. Someone, perhaps Mary Dyer, noticed and brought her a chair.

Gratefully, she sat down, ready to try again. She mentioned a man and a woman in the Bible who'd taught another man. The example she knew was weak, but it was all she had.

Now Winthrop grew sarcastic. "See how your argument stands," he said acidly. "Priscilla, with her husband, took Apollo home to instruct him

66

privately. Therefore Mistress Hutchinson without her husband may teach sixty or eighty." The governor's tart remark brought a sour smile of appreciation to Reverend Symmes's face.

Once more she tried to justify the innocence of her meetings. "I call them not," she said simply. "But if they come to me, I may instruct them."

"Yet you show not a rule," Winthrop insisted yet again.

"I have shown you two places in scripture."

"But neither of them will suit your practice," he said, shaking his head.

Anne Hutchinson could be sarcastic too. "Must I show my name written therein?"

At this there were angry rumbles among the members of the Court. Winthrop decided he had heard enough from Mistress Hutchinson on this point. He told her pointblank that the reason she could hold no further meetings was because the colony's leaders forbade her to do so.

He informed her that no one had the right to set up any practices not authorized by the colony's leaders. "We must therefore put this course away from you or restrain you from maintaining it."

This was authority of too high a hand for Anne's taste. She decided to quote his own principle back to him. "If you have a rule for it from God's word, you may."

Again angry rumblings swept through the meetinghouse. Surely this insolent women needed to be put in her place. Eyebrows drawn together, a frowning Winthrop glared at Anne Hutchinson. "We are *your* judges, and not you *ours,* and we must compel you to it."

Anne refused to be humbled. "If it please you by authority to put it down, I will freely let you, for I am subject to your authority." In other words, she'd bow before his power as governor, but not concede that he was right.

Winthrop was winning this contest of wills, but barely. And only because of the power of his office, not the power of his arguments.

Deputy-Governor Dudley, who thought Winthrop had a tendency to be too easy on sinners, broke in. "I would go a little higher with Mistress Hutchinson," he said impatiently.

One by one, he listed the most serious charges against her. She had been a source of disturbance ever since she'd arrived. In fact, even before she'd arrived. (Here he nodded toward Reverend

Symmes.) She had perverted the minds of a great number of people with her opinions. And worst of all, she'd defamed the ministers by saying they "preached a Covenant of Works and only Mr. Cotton a Covenant of Grace."

At these words, a few members of the Court, though not Dudley, turned to look in John Cotton's direction. But Cotton seemed not to notice, as if someone else's name had been mentioned, not his own.

In order to prove this last charge, the Court would need two witnesses to swear they had heard Anne Hutchinson say this in public. But Anne was certain she had never said those words, at least not publicly.

"Did I ever say they preached a Covenant of Works?" she demanded of Dudley.

Dudley gave a sly reply. "If they do not preach a Covenant of Grace clearly,"—which Anne acknowledged she had said—then it must follow that "they preach a Covenant of Works."

This was jumping to a false conclusion that Anne wouldn't allow. "No, Sir," she protested heatedly. "One may preach a Covenant of Grace more clearly than another. *So* I said."

But Dudley was a hound who would have his

fox. "I will make it plain. You did say that the ministers did preach a Covenant of Works. And," he added, "you said they were not able ministers of the New Testament, but Mr. Cotton only."

Anne noticed that Dudley's words were making Thomas Welde and a few other ministers uncomfortable. Obviously, that "private" meeting she'd had with the ministers the year before hadn't been so private after all. One or more of the ministers had reported to Dudley and the magistrates what she'd said that day.

Anne's eyes flashed. "It is one thing," she said scornfully, "for me to come before a public magistracy and there to speak what they would have me speak." She turned to face the ministers. "And another," she continued bitterly, "when a man comes to me in a way of friendship privately." She spat out the last words in full rage. "There is difference in that!"

Dudley looked unconcerned. Winthrop shrugged, saying, "What if the matter be all one?"

The ministers held an embarrassed silence. Then Reverend Hugh Peter stood up. First he assured the Court, which needed no such assurance, that the ministers didn't want to be thought "informers against the gentlewoman." Then he told all.

He said that at the meeting he'd asked Anne Hutchinson what the difference was between Mr. Cotton and themselves. "She answered that he preaches the Covenant of Grace and you the Covenant of Works and that you are not able ministers of the New Testament."

Angrily, Anne asked John Wilson to produce the notes Thomas Welde had made of the meeting. Then the Court could see that she hadn't said what Hugh Peter claimed. Wilson quietly reported that he no longer had the notes.

Instead, one after another, the ministers backed up Hugh Peter's version.

Now Mr. Dudley accused her of saying other things at that meeting, things she also denied saying. But she really couldn't remember everything that had or hadn't been said that day. The meeting had taken place over a year ago. Her notes on it were at home. She racked her brain trying to remember exactly what it was she *had* said. Then perhaps she could refute the ministers' accusations with some degree of certainty.

But the day was drawing to a close. It was growing too dark to see. Governor Winthrop called a halt to the questioning. They would continue in the morning.

That night, Anne sat in the main room of her

darkened house and pored over her notes. Light from the fire flickered over the walls. For the first time that day, Anne was in a warm place. But she scarcely noticed whether she was cold or warm. She was too excited by the information she found in her notes.

Plainly there were differences between what she'd said at the meeting and what the ministers claimed she'd said. Now she had the proof she needed to show the Court that she was innocent. She went to sleep at last feeling a little easier in her mind. Not only would her notes prove the ministers weren't telling the whole truth, but she'd even formed a plan for making them admit as much.

7 Speaking Out

The next morning Anne again made the long, difficult journey from Boston to Newtown. But this time facing the bitter cold, the ice-cloaked river, the treacherous ladders, the dim and smelly meetinghouse seemed easier. As she strode to the front of the room, her step was lively, her eyes bright and sure. Armed now with her notes, she again sat facing her accusers ranged along the table.

Again she met their stony gazes. After Winthrop finished summing up the case against her so far, she spoke. According to her notes, she said, the facts were not exactly as the ministers had recalled yesterday.

The night before she had thought of a way to force their memories to more accurate recollection. Now she would present it. She pointed out to the Court that the ministers were hardly impartial witnesses in the case. However, there was a way to insure they told the truth. She took a deep breath. "I desire they may speak upon oath."

Speak upon oath! The Court was indignant. Was she calling the ministers liars? "A sign it is," huffed Mr. Endicott, of "what respect she hath for their words."

The first part of Anne Hutchinson's plan wasn't working. Mr. Dudley obviously felt no obligation to compel a table full of ministers to swear to the truth of what they said. So when none offered to take an oath, he simply changed the subject. Mistress Hutchinson had said she had witnesses. Where were they? He didn't see any.

"If you will not call them in," she returned coolly, "that is nothing to me."

"Let her witnesses be called," Dudley cried out.

But Anne's witnesses were not to be allowed to say anything the Court didn't want to hear. Her friend Mr. Coggeshall was the first. "Will you, Mr.

Coggeshall," Winthrop asked him, "say that she did not say so?"

"Yes I dare say that she did not say all that which they lay against her."

At that, the hotheaded Reverend Peter burst out, "How dare you look into the Court to say such a word!"

His words were clearly intended to silence Coggeshall and any other friendly witnesses. Mr. Coggeshall looked uncertainly around the room. Then, with a sigh, he gave in. "Mr. Peter takes it upon him to forbid me. I shall be silent."

Mr. Leverett, Anne's next witness, cautiously reported that Mrs. Hutchinson had said the other ministers did not preach a Covenant of Grace as clearly as Mr. Cotton did.

Now John Cotton came forward as Anne's third witness. At William Colburn's suggestion he had been allowed to sit beside her since the questioning of witnesses began. Her early morning confidence had been shaken by the Court's refusal to put the ministers under oath. Now John Cotton was her only hope. Her heart began to race. Surely she could count on her teacher to stand by her. Surely.

Under Anne's trusting gaze, Cotton began, in

his usual mild and reasonable way, by saying that he hadn't expected to be called as a witness, so he really hadn't tried to remember what had happened at the meeting with the ministers. But he did remember Mrs. Hutchinson being asked to explain why she thought the other ministers didn't preach as clearly as he did. She'd replied, he said, that while the others relied upon works, he himself preached "upon free grace without a work or without a respect to a work."

He added that, at the time, the other ministers had seemed very satisfied with her answers. They'd said they wouldn't believe reports about her so easily again. "And I must say," he concluded, a little more firmly now and his eyes glancing in Anne's direction, "that I did not find her saying they were under a Covenant of Works, nor that she said they did preach a Covenant of Works."

Anne Hutchinson sighed with relief. The rapid beating of her heart slowed down. There it was. Her teacher had stood by her. Anne cast a grateful look at Cotton. He and he alone had told the truth plainly.

But Reverend Peter probed further. Didn't Mr. Cotton remember that she'd said the other ministers couldn't preach a Covenant of Grace?

"That she said you could not preach a Covenant of Grace," he repeated before answering firmly, "I do not remember such a thing."

Now Anne Hutchinson's accusers were troubled. They cast quick glances at each other. Winthrop drummed his fingers nervously against the table top. No one could doubt John Cotton's word, even though it went against what the others had said. Mr. Dudley again reminded Cotton that his fellow ministers had given a different report. "They affirm that Mistress Hutchinson did say they were not able ministers of the New Testament."

"I do not remember it," Cotton stated.

Would Cotton's refusal to support the accusations of the other ministers be enough to save Anne Hutchinson? Nothing was clear. Cotton remembered one thing, the other ministers something else. The Court would decide.

But first Anne Hutchinson asked to speak for herself. And she would speak plainly, explaining what she believed and why she believed it.

When she was yet in England, she began, she'd read in the Bible this passage: "He that denies Jesus Christ to be come in the flesh is the antichrist."[9] From this, she said, she'd concluded that whoever didn't preach the Covenant of Grace had the spirit of the antichrist.

"And ever since," she continued, "I bless the Lord, he hath let me see which was the clear ministry and which the wrong."

She looked squarely at her accusers. "Now," she said, "if you do condemn me for speaking what in my conscience I know to be truth, I must commit myself unto the Lord."

The Court was curious. How did Mistress Hutchinson know it to be the truth? From the voice of the spirit, she answered.

One of the judges, Mr. Nowell, asked her, "How did you know that that was the spirit?"

"How did Abraham know that it was God that bid him offer his son?" she replied.

At this, Dudley looked up quickly. Was she comparing herself with Abraham? "By an immediate voice?" he suggested. He held his breath.

"So to me by an immediate revelation!"

Now she had done it! If she was claiming that God spoke to her directly, then Anne Hutchinson had condemned herself out of her own mouth.

_____

[9] an enemy of Jesus Christ; a person of great evil

80

Dudley jerked himself upright. "How by an immediate revelation?" he demanded to know.

"By the voice of his own spirit to my soul."

There was a stir all up and down the table. Gasps could be heard from the crowd on the benches. Holding such a belief was far worse than even slandering the ministers had been. Cotton turned to Anne Hutchinson with a look of disbelief.

The judges and ministers barely heard the rest of her speech. It scarcely mattered now. It was a Puritan article of faith that God no longer spoke to people directly, as he had in Biblical days. If he did, anyone could claim to know the truth and the community of saints would dissolve. The only way to discover what God wanted was by reading the Bible and listening to the ministers.

Anne Hutchinson ignored the uproar she'd caused and ended her speech with a warning. The Court, she said, was doing "as much as in you lies to put the Lord Jesus Christ from you, and, if you go on in this course you begin, you will bring a curse upon you and your posterity. *And the mouth of the Lord hath spoken it."*

The judges couldn't believe it. Now she was threatening them with a curse! No doubt she believed in miracles too. How else did she think to be acquitted after what she'd just said?

"Daniel was delivered by a miracle," Winthrop scoffed. "Do you think to be delivered so too?"

"I do here speak it before the Court," she answered, her voice on fire with the passion of truth-telling. "I look that the Lord should deliver me by his providence."

Now Mr. Endicott eyed John Cotton, who was still standing next to her. Perhaps this woman's teacher wasn't as above suspicion as everyone presumed. "I desire you to give your judgment of Mistress Hutchinson," he said to Cotton.

John Cotton was not easily moved by the passions of the moment. As usual he tried to draw a fine line to separate truth from error. "If she doth expect a deliverance in a way of Providence—then I cannot deny it," he began in measured words. "If it be by way of a miracle, then I would suspect it."

"Do you believe that her revelations are true?" Dudley demanded impatiently.

Possibly, in a certain sense, they were, he answered.

Now Endicott was fit to be tied. Enough. He wanted a plain answer. He wanted to know, "Whether you do witness for her or against her?"

But Cotton's reply remained evasive to their ears. In some senses it would be all right to look to Providence for deliverance. In other senses it wouldn't.

Annoyed at Cotton's persistent hair-splitting, Dudley rapped out, "Sir, you weary me and do not satisfy me."

Other members of the Court, astounded by Cotton's lingering support for Anne Hutchinson, began to move in on him. "It is a great burden to us," said one, "that we differ from Mr. Cotton and that he should justify these revelations. I would entreat him to answer."

But Governor Winthrop quickly put a stop to this line of questioning. John Cotton was far too important a member of the colony to be lost in this controversy. There must be no chance of his sharing Anne Hutchinson's fate. "Mr. Cotton is not called to answer anything," he pronounced. "But we are to deal with the party standing before us."

They dealt with her swiftly, though a few of her remaining supporters protested. Mr. Coddington said, "I do not see any clear witness against her, and you know it is a rule of the Court that no man may be a judge and an accuser too." But Winthrop brushed this objection aside.

Then a Mr. Stoughton pointed out that, "she hath not been formally convicted as others are by witness upon oath."

Abruptly, Winthrop selected two ministers and had them raise their hands and take the oath. Both testified that Anne Hutchinson had said that the ministers were not able ministers of the New Testament.

Winthrop took a show of hands. Should Mistress Hutchinson be found guilty? All but three of the magistrates held up their hands. Then Winthrop pronounced sentence.

"Mistress Hutchinson, the sentence of the Court you hear is that you are banished from out of our jurisdiction as being a woman not fit for our society, and are to be imprisoned till the Court shall send you away."

Anne stood straight before the Court, still undefeated. "I desire to know wherefore I am banished," she demanded.

"Say no more," Winthrop shot back at her, "the Court knows wherefore and is satisfied."

8 By Way of Questions

Anne Hutchinson spent the four months of her imprisonment in Roxbury in the home of Joseph Welde, the brother of Pastor Welde. The only visitors she was allowed were her family and members of the clergy. She had plenty of time to read the Bible and think. She began to doubt and question many of the truths of her religion, especially those that dealt with death and immortality.

The ministers who came to visit claimed to be concerned for the state of her soul. They encouraged her to share her doubts with them. Lonely and confused, she poured out her heart, hoping that now that the battle was over they might help put her troubled mind to rest.

In the meantime, many of her supporters were punished—dragged before the Court to be banished or fined or deprived of the vote. Others escaped punishment by renouncing their former beliefs.

When spring came Anne Hutchinson was taken to the Boston church to be dealt with "in a church way" before she was banished from the colony forever. By now her former supporters were either gone or humbled. Her husband was away, looking for a new home for them outside the colony. As she walked up the aisle to face her accusers, she saw only a few friendly faces in the congregation. Her son Edward and his wife, her daughter Faith and her husband were there. Her friend Mary Dyer, seated near the front, smiled brave encouragement.

Once again, Anne discovered, the ministers she had trusted had betrayed her. The doubts and questions she had talked to them about during her imprisonment were now charged against her as additional errors. She protested that these were only questions she had raised, not her actual opinions. It did no good.

"I would have this congregation know," the Reverend Shephard intoned, "that the vilest errors that were ever brought into the church was brought in by way of questions."

For the next nine hours the ministers, John Cotton among them, questioned her and argued with her. The physical and mental agony of this ordeal was small compared to the pain of realizing that even her beloved teacher had now turned against her. In the gathering darkness, the members of her church voted on whether or not Anne Hutchinson should be admonished, that is, publicly scolded, for her errors.

Her son Edward and Thomas Savage, her son-in-law, both protested. This caused a problem since all church decisions had to be unanimous. It was suggested that the two young men be considered for admonishment as well, in which case, of course, they couldn't vote on the matter.

Pastor Wilson thought that a splendid idea. The church then voted to admonish Anne Hutchinson and the two young men. The job of administering the public scolding was given to John Cotton.

For over twenty years, Anne had listened to Cotton's teachings. She had followed him across the ocean to the New World. He had been her inspiration—the one who taught her what she believed. Now, sick and exhausted, she stood with her head bowed before him as he detailed her errors and the harm she had caused to the community of saints. Her teachings, he said, were dangerous. Her doubts would lead others to sin.

Heart-stricken, she listened as he spoke the dreadful words. "I do admonish you, and also charge you in the name of Christ Jesus, in whose place I stand, that you would sadly consider the just hand of God against you, the great hurt you have done to the churches, the great dishonor you have brought to Jesus Christ, and the evil that you have done to many a poor soul."

Anne Hutchinson spent the next week in John Cotton's home. During that time she agreed that all the doubts and questions she had were unfounded. She returned to the meetinghouse the following Thursday and humbly read her retraction. In her defense she said only that, "I did not hold any of these things before my imprisonment."

The ministers refused to accept that. She had held, they insisted, these opinions for a long time. They called her a liar, a "notorious impostor." John Cotton said, "I think we are bound upon this ground to remove her from us, seeing she doth prevaricate[10] in her words."

---

[10] lie

Pastor Wilson read the words of excommunication. "In the name of our Lord Jesus Christ, I do cast you out and deliver you up to Satan and account you from this time forth to be a heathen and a publican. I command you in the name of Christ Jesus and of this church, as a leper to withdraw yourself out of the congregation."

The family of saints that had welcomed her a few years before was now shutting the door on her.

For a moment Anne Hutchinson stood still, listening to the silence. Then she turned to face the congregation. Head high, she walked down the aisle. Mary Dyer rose from her seat and slipped her arm into Anne's. Together they walked out of the church into the fresh clean air of spring.

Epilogue

In March 1638, the Hutchinsons began a new life in Rhode Island, helping to found the settlement of Portsmouth. When William died four years later, Anne took her six youngest children to New York. There in the late summer of 1643, she and all but one of her children were killed in an Indian raid near Pelham Bay. Anne Hutchinson was 52. Susanna, the only survivor of the raid, was taken captive. When she was rescued several years later, she strongly resisted returning to the English settlements.

Conflicts continued to plague the Puritan colony. Mary Dyer, who had followed Anne to Rhode Island, returned to England in 1650 and became a member of the Society of Friends, or Quakers. She returned to New England, was banished for her beliefs, and later hanged in Boston for refusing to accept her banishment.

The trial of Anne Hutchinson shows what happens when consciences clash and there is no room for compromise. None of the Puritans, not John Winthrop nor Anne Hutchinson, not Zachariah Symmes nor John Wheelwright, believed in compromise in matters of conscience.

They *did* believe in liberty of conscience—the right to follow one's own conscience—but if what you believed differed from the established beliefs of the church and state, you were required to keep your beliefs to yourself or leave. If you failed to do either you could be forced to leave, as Anne and her family were, or be killed, as Mary Dyer eventually was. In conflicts between the individual and the government (or between the individual and the community), the individual usually lost.

Nearly 150 years after the death of Anne Hutchinson, the Bill of Rights became part of the United States Constitution. In the First Amendment is contained the guarantee that the government shall make no law that interferes with an individual's religious beliefs, right to speak freely, or right to meet peacefully in public.

This guarantee is the only protection an individual has against the power of the government. It is also the only protection the few have against the many. The First Amendment allows us to speak and act as our individual consciences tell us. It also gives us the necessary room to disagree peacefully.

But the Bill of Rights is only a piece of paper. It requires the good faith of the American people to work. We cannot let people be silenced simply because we disagree with what they have to say. We don't have to like what others say when they exercise their First Amendment rights, we only have to tolerate it. In order to guarantee your rights, you must protect the rights of others.

Afterword

Information about the events in this story comes mainly from the transcript of Anne Hutchinson's trial and from John Winthrop's journals and letters. All words shown in quotation marks were actually spoken by the people in the story. Speeches and thoughts not in quotation marks are paraphrases based on the beliefs, values, thoughts, attitudes, and opinions held by those involved.

Notes

Pages 1–4 Cotton's escape and the departure of the *Griffin* are mentioned in Governor Winthrop's journal, but some of the details—a pat of the hand and a seaward glance—have been made up. Another Puritan minister, Mr. Thomas Hooker, also boarded ship at the same place but not necessarily at the same time as the Cottons. Sarah Cotton did give birth aboard the *Griffin*. The Cottons named their infant son Seaborn.

Page 2 Many of the Puritans came from the part of England around old Boston, where Cotton's church was located. Boston, Massachusetts is named after this town in England.

Page 6 Details of the provisions the new colonists

brought to America were taken from a letter John Winthrop wrote to his wife, Margaret (who wasn't able to accompany him in 1630). In the letter, Winthrop advised his wife on what to bring.

Page 10 The Biblical text on which John Cotton preached that day in 1630 was from the Second Book of Samuel, Chapter 7, Verse 10: "Moreover I will appoint a place for my people Israel, and I will plant them, that they may dwell in a place of their own, and move no more." Winthrop had taken this verse about the Hebrews and the land of Israel to heart. For him, America was the new Israel and the Puritans the new Chosen People.

Pages 12–13 Anne Hutchinson's thoughts at this time were later reported by her during her trial in New England.

Pages 14–15 These are the names and ages of the Hutchinson children at the time of their departure from England: Edward (already in America), 21 or 22; Richard, 18; Faith, about 16; Bridget, about 15; Francis, 13 or 14; Samuel, 9; Anne, 8; Mary, 6; Katherine, 4; William, almost 3; and Susanna, 8 months.

Pages 15–16 The routine details of life aboard the *Griffin* on this particular crossing were not recorded. However Winthrop's journal gave details of shipboard life during the *Lady Arbella's* crossing in 1630. I've assumed that daily activities aboard the *Griffin* weren't much different than those aboard the *Lady Arbella*. Therefore, I've used Winthrop's descriptions to set scenes and describe routine tasks.

The fish tubs were used to keep fish alive until they were to be cooked and eaten. Punishments like those described were common in New England, as well as at sea.

Pages 18–22 Although the exact words of Anne Hutchinson's conversations weren't recorded, it is known that she had many such discussions aboard ship and held the beliefs stated here. Symmes himself reported that Anne had argued with him. He described what she said, including the two quotations that particularly maddened him.

Page 28 The climate of North America produces a much more colorful fall foliage than the English climate does. The spectacle of the autumnal changing of the leaves was often commented on.

Page 28 The Puritans changed the names of the days of the week: Sunday became First-day, Monday was Second-day, and so forth.

Page 29 When John Cotton, the leading Puritan minister of his time, arrived in Boston, the church members naturally wanted him to be their minister. This spot was already filled by John Wilson, and no one wished to turn him out. The solution was to appoint Cotton to the position of church teacher. Supposedly, John Wilson, as pastor, was to inspire and correct the congregation, while Cotton, as teacher, was to instruct. In practice, however, the duties of both men were quite similar.

Page 37 John Wilson's wife had originally refused to make the journey to New England with her husband. Now Wilson was returning to England in order to convince her to come to New England with him.

Page 39 The General Court was the assembly of leaders of the Massachusetts Bay Colony. It included two representatives, or deputies, from each town. To vote, one had to be a man who owned land and was also a church member. Because this didn't include women or children, and many men were not church members, the voters made up a small percentage of the colony's population. Still, even with its limits, it was a representative democracy, which was rare for the time.

Page 40 In the 1600s, most women gave birth at home with the help of a midwife, a woman who assists in childbirth. Doctors or surgeons weren't involved, which, given the nature of medical expertise at the time, is probably just as well. In addition to the midwife, other women of the neighborhood would gather at the house to give additional help and comfort. Anne Hutchinson learned her midwife and nursing skills in England. She performed this service out of charity, not for pay.

Pages 40–41 According to Winthrop, Mary Dyer was "a very proper and fair woman" who had "a very proud spirit" and was "much addicted to revelations." I can't be sure that Mary was the friend who told Anne what the other women were thinking, but since she seems to have been Anne's closest friend, I've assumed that she was.

Page 44 As the wife of a prosperous cloth merchant, Anne was one of the colony's leading citizens and entitled to be called Mistress. Jane Hawkins, as one of the common people, was called Goodwife, often shortened to Goody. The equivalent terms for men were Mister and Goodman.

Pages 45–46 One Puritan, a certain Edward Johnson, said of William Dinely that "So soon as any were set down in his chair, he would commonly be cutting off their hair and the truth together." A "ninneversity" was a joke word he made up, meaning a university for ninnies. "Blackcoats" was a slang term for ministers, who frequently wore long black coats. The fact that Dinely was both a barber and a surgeon, and a barber first, tells you all you need to know of the quality of surgery at the time.

Page 48 John Wheelwright was married to Mary Hutchinson, William's sister. In England, he had been a vicar of Bilby, a town one mile away from Anne Hutchinson's hometown of Alford in Lincolnshire.

Pages 50–54 Besides Cotton, the ministers present at this meeting were John Wilson, Hugh Peter of Salem, Zachariah Symmes of Charlestown, George Phillips of Roxbury, Thomas Shepard of Cambridge, and John Eliot and Thomas Welde of Roxbury.

Pages 54–56 Things reached such a state between the Hutchinsonians and the rest of the colony that when war broke out between the Pequot Indians and the New England colonists in 1637, few Hutchinsonians answered Governor Winthrop's call for volunteers. Pastor Wilson was appointed military chaplain of the colonial militia. When he left with the troops almost no one from his congregation in Boston would even say goodbye to him.

Pages 61–62 Ministers taking part in a Court proceeding was not odd. There was no seperation of church and state in Puritan New England. The Puritans believed that a good society was run according to the laws of God. The Bible, as interpreted by

100

the ministers and magistrates, gave them civil laws as well as religious laws.

Page 65 Chapter 2 of Titus reads, "The aged women likewise, that they in behavior as becometh holiness, not false accusers, not given to much wine, teachers of good things; that they may teach the young women to be sober, to love their husbands, to love their children, to be discreet, chaste keepers at home, good, obedient to their own husbands . . . ." Because the verse included the idea of women serving as teachers, Anne offered it to Winthrop as proof of Biblical approval of her meetings. He rejected it because he saw it as limited to older women teaching younger women to be good wives and mothers, not as authorizing religious instruction by women.

Page 80 The story of Abraham and Isaac is told in the Book of Genesis of the Bible. In order to test his faith, God appeared to Abraham, instructing him to kill his son, Isaac. Abraham, pained by his instructions but ready to obey God, reached for his knife before God sent a ram to take Isaac's place. The Puritans believed that such direct communication between people and God no longer occurred.

Joan Kane Nichols lives in New Orleans, Louisiana. She is the author of the children's books *All But the Right Folks* and *New Orleans*.